I0413101

NIST GCR 09-924

Determination of Montmorillonite Nanocomposite Aggregation Rates Using Real Time X-Ray Diffraction Techniques at High Temperatures

Holly A. Stretz
Department of Chemical Engineering
Tennessee Technological University
Cookeville, TN 38501

National Institute of
Standards and Technology
U.S. Department of Commerce

NIST GCR 09-924

Determination of Montmorillonite Nanocomposite Aggregation Rates Using Real Time X-Ray Diffraction Techniques at High Temperatures

Prepared for
U.S. Department of Commerce
Building and Fire Research Laboratory
National Institute of Standards and Technology
Gaithersburg, MD 20899-8665

By
Holly A. Stretz
Department of Chemical Engineering
Tennessee Technological University
Cookeville, TN 38501

April 2009

U.S. Department of Commerce
Gary Locke, Secretary

National Institute of Standards and Technology
Patrick D. Gallagher, Acting Director

NIST Grant Number 70NANB7H6006

Year One: Final Report

Determination of Montmorillonite Nanocomposite Aggregation Rates Using Real Time X-Ray Diffraction Techniques at High Temperatures

Holly A. Stretz

Department of Chemical Engineering

Tennessee Technological University

Cookeville, TN 38501

September 2008

TABLE OF CONTENTS

Executive Summary

In October 1998 a NIST-industrial consortium convened to study mechanisms by which montmorillonite clays afford fire resistance to composites formed from various polymers and montmorillonite. This committee concluded that a clay-reinforced carbonaceous char is produced during the combustion of such nanocomposites, and this "barrier layer" protects the underlying part[1]. Since that time researchers have shown that montmorillonite particles in polymer-based nanocomposites will aggregate under fire conditions (see Kashiwagi et al.[2] and Gilman et al.[3]), and Lewin et al. have suggested that the particles may in some cases migrate to the surface[4]. All of this evidence implies that self-assembly of the nanoparticles is occurring as the part burns.

The current work explored how choice of surfactant, fire temperature and processing pressure affect the assembly process for particles in the barrier layer. The underlying assumption was that the nano-structure of the ceramic portion of the barrier layer would affect flammability, and this assumption was explored as well.

In the original research plan, the goals in this first year were to compare how self assembly rates were affected by: (1) Surfactant, (2) Polymer, (3) Initial state of dispersion and (4) Melt rheology.

Characterization of these structural changes was accomplished using high temperature real-time X-ray diffraction (HTXRD), a technique available to TTU researchers on a limited basis through the Oak Ridge National Laboratory User Program. Since access to the aforementioned instrument was productive but time-restricted, TTU researchers corroborated the XRD results by investigating a new structure-sensitive detection technique based on gaseous permeability of the formed barrier layer. In addition some early computational work is presented herein to test/validate our primary assumption, that structure of the barrier layer affects flammability.

The most important conclusions/results from this year's work are summarized below:

1. Effect of surfactant on barrier layer structural formation in virgin organoclays.

    a. All organoclays up to 800°C exhibited a 16Å phase.

    b. All organoclays exhibited a temperature-dependent "collapsing" phase.

c. Thermal stability of the surfactant (TGA) correlated with the onset of the structural "collapse" (XRD).

d. Chemical changes (TGA) occur at lower temperatures than structural changes (XRD).

e. Nanomer I44.P appears structurally stable up to $800^{\circ}C$, suggesting production of an aerogel on heating.

2. Effect of pressure on barrier layer formation in virgin organoclays.

a. In the absence of pressure Nanomer I44.P appeared to produce an aerogel, while Cloisite 20A did not. Under pressure, however, both organoclays produced the same collapsed phase.

b. TEM images of the collapsed phase in Cloisite 20A show an interesting trend towards a hybrid phase with alternating interlayers, or "staged heterostructures."

3. Significance of permeability: a bulk scale test for micron-scale structural changes.

a. Five composite models all predicted higher relative permeability than experimentally observed relative peak mass loss rate (RPMLR).

b. The Cussler model (random arrays) was closest predictor.

c. Fluxes of Ar through 0.4 mm thickness of organoclay ash averaged 0.140 $mol/m^{2} \cdot sec$.

d. On heating/pressing, Cloisite 20A an permeability increased. This data is not consistent with compaction of void spaces, but is consistent with reduced filler particle aspect ratio.

4. Future Plans

a. A multidisciplinary team composed of a ceramic/aggregate sintering expert (J. Biernacki) and a nanocomposite fire performance expert (H. Stretz) will study the deformation of the organoclay ash. Analog chemistry from aggregate sintering will aid development of nanocomposite barrier layers with higher mechanical strength.

b. Future XRD studies will be enabled by the planned purchase of a P'Analytical XRD Diffractometer at TTU, installation by summer 2009.

5. Outcomes

a. One domestic graduate student, Mr. Brent Fox, received his Master's in Chemical Engineering, 12-2008, and is now employed with Jacobs Engineering in Houston, TX.

b. Presentation: Stretz, H. A., "Nanocomposite Fire Performance: Contribution of Montmorillonite Barrier Layer," Samuel Ginn College of Engineering Chemical Engineering Seminar Series, Auburn University, 10-17-2007, INVITED.

c. Presentation: Fox, J. B., Stretz, H. A., Payzant, A., Meisner, R., "Aggregation of nanoparticles using real-time high temperature x-ray diffraction," *Polymer Materials Science and Engineering Preprints*, ACS, 04-2008.

d. Paper: Fox, B., Stretz, H. A., Payzant, A., Meisner, R., "Formation of Nanostructure During Gasification of Montmorillonite Organoclays," in draft for *Small*.

e. Paper: Fox, B., Stretz, H. A., "Permeability as an Analog to Flammability in Montmorillonite Organoclay Ash" in draft for *Polymers in Advanced Technology*.

1. Introduction

1.1. Overview of experimental timeline

The initial proposal described a set of goals for XRD analysis which required one year's pursuit. They were:

-- to compare how nanoparticle self assembly rates were affected by the: (1) surfactant, (2) polymer, (3) initial state of dispersion and (4) melt rheology.

The projected direction of this work was revised slightly to accommodate the ORNL User Program queue. Given unscheduled instrument (XRD) downtime, the contingency research plan was to investigate the validity of using permeability as a detector for nano-structural changes in the degraded clay using XRD information for corroboration. Research results for item (1) in the original plan are reported herein. Additional research results from the permeability studes are reported as well. A no-cost extension of three months was granted.

1.2. Revised goals

The updated goals of the investigation address three questions:

- Does surfactant choice affect the evolution of nanostructure changes in organoclays at fire temperatures?
- Does processing pressure affect the evolution of nanostructure changes in organoclays at fire temperatures?
- Do temperature/pressure-induced structural changes in the organoclay correlate with changes in Ar permeability of the organoclay? If so, do observed mass transport rates validate the concept that mass loss rate should be reduced by the tortuous path offered by the forming barrier layer?

2. Experimental

2.1. Overview

The materials used in this study benchmark certain novel measurement techniques, and therefore the choice of materials intentionally matches those reported in selected recent publications. Two of the novel techniques employed here for detecting nano-scale structural changes in the forming barrier layer were: high temperature X-ray diffraction (HTXRD) and Ar permeability of the barrier layer. These two methods are summarized/described below.

XRD experiments were used to assess aggregation of organoclay materials using both parallel beam geometry and a sample oven which allows the sample to be heated during scanning without moving or otherwise disturbing the sample. This specialized equipment eliminated the possibility of certain artifacts expected to arise if the fragile organoclay ash sample had to be handled between scans. The specialized optics also helped eliminate artifacts due to changes the sample height during degradation.

Permeability was used to assess for changes in the mass transfer rate of the sample (transport of gases) due to the presence of a barrier layer. This should correlate to the reduction in the mass loss rate and therefore correlate structural changes with an improvement in flammability. **This novel method provides us with a multi-scale approach for analyzing the structure of the barrier layer upon degradation** by relating a bulk property (permeability) to a nanoscale property (XRD response).

2.2. Materials and Processing

All materials were used as received, and are described in Table I.

Four MMT organoclays were used throughout the course of this work. Three of these, referred to here as $M_3(HT)$, $M_2(HT)_2$, and $M(HT)_3$, and were obtained from Southern Clay Products. These organoclays consist of MMT modified with quaternary ammonium ions with varying structures as surfactants. $M_3(HT)$ is an experimental MMT organo-modified clay with a hydrogenated tallow trimethyl quaternary ammonium ion surfactant. Cloisite® 20A ($M_2(HT)_2$) is a commercial MMT organo-modified clay with a di(hydrogenated tallow) dimethyl quaternary ammonium surfactant. $M(HT)_3$ is an experimental organo-modified bentonite clay with a tri (hydrogenated tallow) methyl quaternary ammonium surfactant. The fourth organoclay, Nanomer® I-44P, produced by Nanocor Company in Arlington Heights, IL, was donated by Dr. Menachem Lewin at Polytechnic University, and its surfactant structure was not provided by the manufacturer.

Petrothene® PP31KK01 is one of the PP homopolymers used for injection molding, and was donated by Equistar Chemicals in Houston, TX. The Petrothene® has a melt flow rate of 5g/10 min. Polybond® X5140 was donated by Dr. Menachem Lewin from Polytechnic University in New York, NY. Polybond® X5140 is a PP homopolymer grafted with 1.5% by weight of maleic anhydride (MA) created by Crompton Corporation.

Table I: Materials Description

Material	Description	Manufacturer
Petrothene® PP31KK01	PP homopolymer	Equistar Chemicals
Polybond® X5140*	PP w/1.5% by maleic anhydride by weight	Crompton Corporation
Nanomer® I-44P*	Montmorillonite organoclay w/ an unknown surfactant	Nanocor Company
$M_3(HT)$	Montmorillonite organoclay w/ a one-tailed surfactant	Southern Clay Products
Cloisite® 20A $(M_2(HT)_2)$	Montmorillonite organoclay w/ a two-tailed surfactant	Southern Clay Products
$M(HT)_3$	Montmorillonite organoclay w/ a three-tailed surfactant	Southern Clay Products
Nitrogen	Compressed N_2	Airgas Company
Air	Compressed air	Airgas Company
Argon	Compressed Argon	Airgas Company
EMbed 812	Four part epoxy	Electron Microscopy Sciences

* Materials supplied by Dr. Menachem Lewin at Polytechnic University New York, NY

The pressure experiments were conducted on a Carver 3850 hot press. The samples were pressed at 250 °C and 6.9 kPa between sheets of aluminum foil and exposed to pressure for one minute, five minute, and ten minute time periods. After the time elapsed for each sample, they were promptly removed from the press and placed in a dessicator until they were sent to Oak Ridge National Labs for XRD analysis.

For nanocomposite samples, the mixing was performed on a DSM 5cm³ twin-screw micro compounder combined with bench-top pneumatic ram injection molding (see figure 1.) Each nanocomposite was compounded as a batch at 200 rpm and 190 °C for 10 minutes. The polymer material was then injected into the 45 °C mold and allowed to cool. The parts were placed in a dessicator. They were milled to approximately 1 mm thickness using a commercial automatic router, with final thickness that of a dime. The milled samples were kept in a dessicator until they were examined at ORNL. Milling to leave only the skin of the injection molded part assured that within that skin the nanostrucuture at the beginning of the XRD experiment exhibited reproducible net orientation.

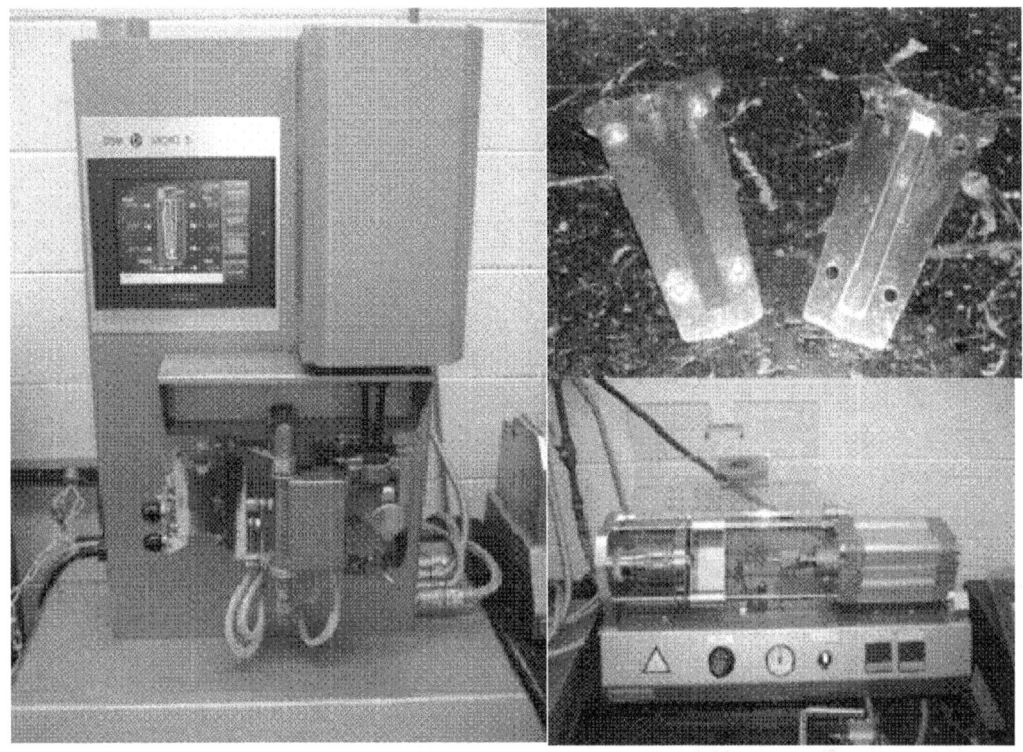

Figure 1: DSM Microcompounder for creating injection molded nanocomposite parts with reproducible initial MMT orientation.

2.3. Characterization

All of the XRD data in this work was obtained at the High Temperature Materials Laboratory located at Oak Ridge National Laboratory (see figure 2.) For initial samples the PI and all authors were present at the time of testing. These samples were analyzed by Dr. R. Meisner on a Philips X'Pert Pro MPD diffractometer using Cu Kα1 radiation at 45 kV and 40 mA. The beam geometry consisted of 0.04 radian soller slits, a parabolic multilayer mirror with a 1/2° fixed slit on the incident beam side, a multi purpose stage, a parallel-plate collimator (0.09°), and a miniprop point detector. The geometry and optics used provide a nearly monochromatic and pseudo-parallel x-ray beam. The pseudo-parallel beam optics make the diffraction scans nearly insensitive to the displacement of the sample within the chamber. For the unmodified organoclays, XRD patterns were collected in air from 25 °C to 850 °C with a temperature ramp of 20 °C per minute and a 30 second hold at temperature prior to initiating the XRD scan. For the composites that were examined in this study, XRD patterns were collected in air or flowing

N_2 from 25 °C to 375 °C with a temperature ramp of 20 °C/ minute and a 30 second hold at temperature prior to initiating the XRD scan.

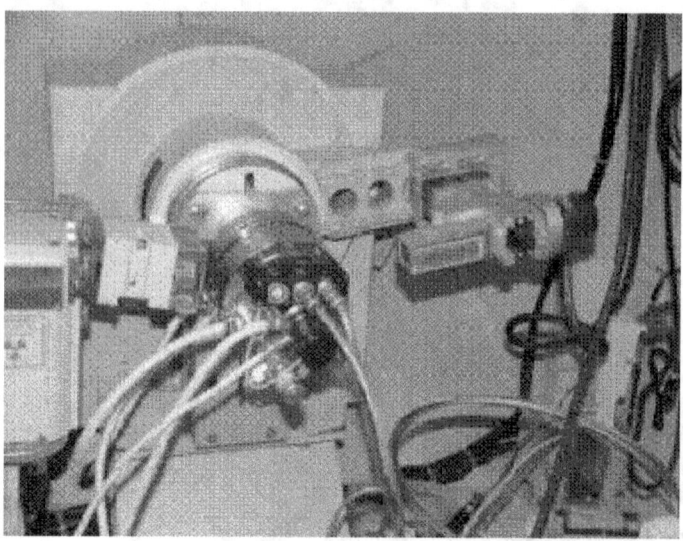

Figure 2: Phillips X'Pert Pro MPD Diffractometer with parallel beam optics, courtesy of Oak Ridge National Laboratory.

The electron microscope photomicrographs were produced at the Coordinated Instrumentation Facility at Tulane University by Dr. Jibao He. The samples were embedded in an epoxy matrix (see Table I), cured and mailed from TTU to Tulane. Dr. He then microtomed the samples. The microscope used was a JEOL 2010 Scanning Transmission Electron Microscope (TEM) with a LaB_6 filament at an electron accelerating voltage of 180 kV. Several images were taken at different magnifications ranging from 400 X to 100,000 X.

The TGA instrument was a TA Instruments model SDT 2960 Simultaneous DSC-TGA. The simultaneous DSC feature was turned off during the running of these experiments. For each organoclay, TGA was conducted for two runs an air atmosphere. The temperature was programmed to increase from room temperature at a rate of $10^{o}C$ per minute to $800^{o}C$ and held for 45 minutes. The 40 mL alumina pans were used. The sample pan was filled approximately halfway and then replaced in the testing chamber for approximately 30 minutes to stabilize the mass prior to testing.

2.4. Permeability
2.4.1. Test Apparatus

The setup consists of a diffusion cell, mass spectrometer, flow controllers, carrier and diffusing gases, and track-etched polycarbonate (TEPC) membranes, and these are diagrammed in figures 3 and 4. The diffusion cell used in these experiments consists of two chambers separated by a membrane. Each of the chambers has an inlet and outlet for the flowing gas. The side in which the carrier gas flows through is designated as the "sample side", while the side in which the diffusing gas flows is designated as the "purge side". A mass-spectrometer was used to detect the permeate gases; a model MG 2100 Gas Analyzer from Monitor Instruments Inc., and was attached to a data acquisition system. There were two Fathom Technologies GR series flow controllers. The flow controller on the purge side, designated as flow controller #1, was set to 30 SCCM and the flow controller on the sample side, designated as flow controller #2, was set to 9.5 SCCM. The carrier gas for the experiments was nitrogen. The diffusing gas for the experimental runs was argon. The membrane supports used in these experiments are highly permeable TEPC membranes from Sterlitech Corporation in Kent, WA. The supports are 47 mm in diameter and have holes etched through them that measure 0.03 µm in diameter throughout the surface of the membrane. All of the components of the setup were connected by 1/8" tubing.

The flow meters that were used in all of the experiments were first calibrated using a bubble flow meter. For flow controller #1, the flow rate was varied from 20 SCCM to 95 SCCM. The flow was timed from the point where the bubble was at the cm³ line to the 30 cm³ line. Flow controller #2 was varied from 3 SCCM to 9.5 SCCM. The flow for this controller was timed from the point where the bubble was at 0 cm³ to 10 cm³.

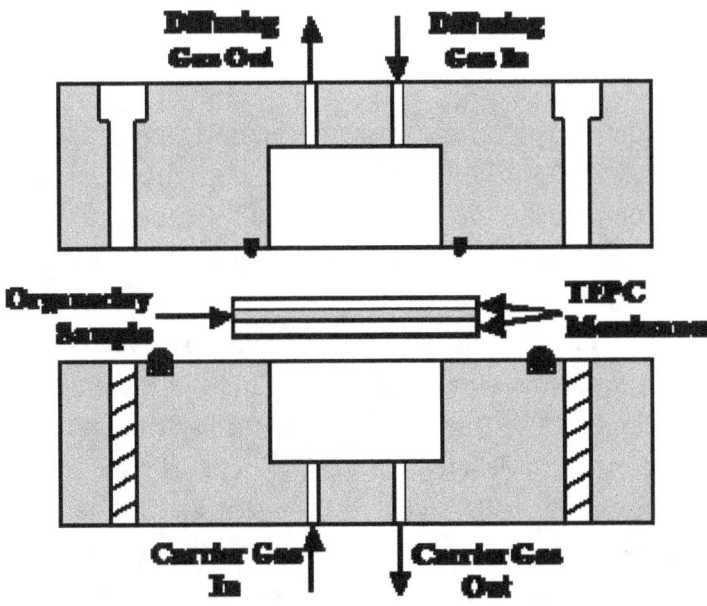

Figure 3: Cross-section of diffusion cell showing detail (not to scale.)

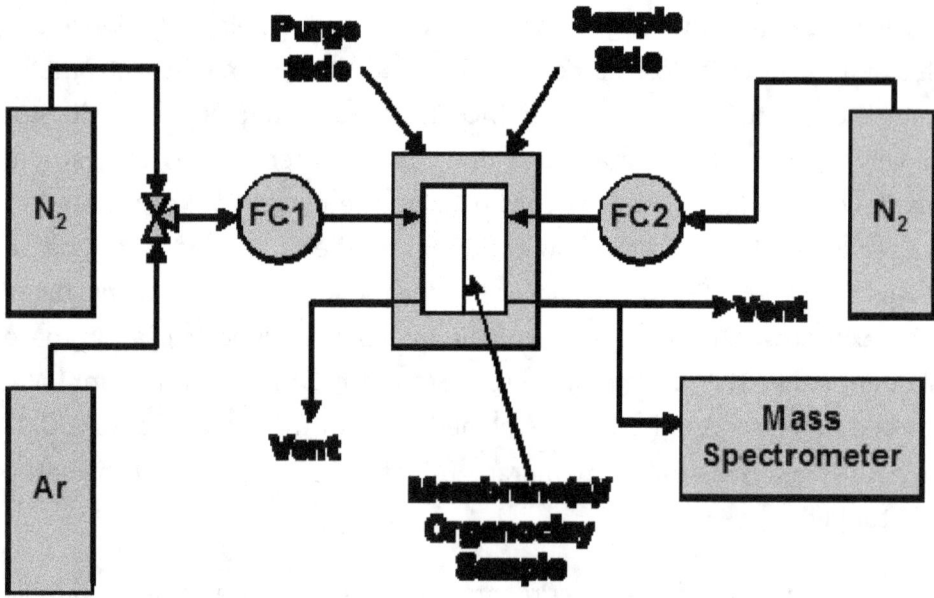

Figure 4: Diagram of permeability test apparatus setup.

2.4.2. Sample preparation for permeability experiments

The degradation of the organoclays was carried out in a Fisher Scientific Isotemp® Programmable Furnace Model 497. The Cloisite® 20A samples were placed in an alumina open topped crucible. The ramp rate for the furnace was set at 20 °C/min up to the operating temperatures. Both the 250 °C and 850 °C samples were held at their set points for 15 minutes after which the temperature was ramped back down to room temperature at 20 °C/min.

The pressed organoclay samples for these experiments were pressed on a Carver 3856 hot press. The temperature was set at 482 °F (250 °C) for both plates. Using a spatula, organoclay was placed on a piece of aluminum foil approximately 8 cm X 8 cm and spread out evenly. Another piece of aluminum foil, which was the same size as the previous piece, was placed on top of the organoclay. The force applied for these analyses was the lowest measureable force on this press, which is 1500 lbs (6672 N). Using an area of 900 cm², the calculated pressure that was applied to the organoclay was 10.8 psi (74.1 kPa). A timer was started and the samples were exposed to pressure for ten minute time periods. After the time elapsed for each sample, they were promptly removed from the press and placed in labeled zip-loc bags in a dessicator. The ash was later scraped into a metal ring mold in the same manner as the sample preparation of organoclays for XRD, except the mold was specific to the diameter of the permeability apparatus. Track etch membranes were used to sandwich the packed ash sample.

3. Results and Discussion

As discussed in the introduction, analyses were organized to attempt to answer three questions. These were:

- How does surfactant affect the evolution of nanostructure changes in organoclays at fire temperatures?
- How does processing pressure affect the evolution of nanostructure changes in organoclays at fire temperatures?
- Do temperature/pressure-induced structural changes in the organoclay correlate with changes in Ar permeability of the organoclays, and if so do observed mass transport rates validate the concept that mass loss rate should be reduced by the tortuous path offered by the forming barrier layer?

The results will be presented to resolve these questions about self-assembly of MMT at high temperatures. **Note that formation of the MMT barrier layer exhibits some behaviors quite similar to the stages seen in sintering/firing of ceramics (such as preparation of fly ash for aggregate).** We believe that **a future study involving a multidisciplinary team** of experts, including an expert in the structure formation of aggregate, will help nanomaterials researchers understand a very important phenomena related to structure and fire performance of nanocomposites: **improving the strength of the barrier layer.**

3.1. Effect of Surfactant on Evolution of Nanostructure in Organoclay at Fire Temperatures

High temperature x-ray diffraction (HTXRD) analysis was used to follow the change in the d_{001} spacing during heating of four MMT organoclays. This type of XRD analysis benefited the study in some important ways. First, the sample is heated in an oven through which the x-rays pass and the sample is held horizontal and stationary during that heating. Therefore the structure of the sample is not potentially disturbed by any attempts to transfer it between isotherms. Secondly, parallel beam optics were used, which prevented alterations or artifacts in the "fingerprint" of the scan due to a potential change in sample height during heating/degradation.

Three organoclays were selected in order to study the effect of surfactant structure on the shift in d_{001} spacing. These surfactants are described in more detail in the experimental section. In summary, $M_3(HT)$ has a single hydrogenated tallow "tail" in the quaternary ammonium ion surfactant, Cloisite® 20A, $M_2(HT)_2$ has two tallow "tails", and $M(HT)_3$ has three tallow "tails". The remainder of the substituents for all three organoclay surfactants were methyl groups.

The HTXRD scans for $M_3(HT)$ are given in figure 5. The initial scan of this organoclay reveals a single peak corresponding to 18.5 Å. Upon heating the single peak is replaced by two peaks. The peak at 16.1 Å remains constant throughout the range of temperatures. As the temperature increases the second peak at 13.2 Å broadens and shifts towards the peak at 9.9 Å seen when the temperature reaches 800 °C, at which point the peak becomes too small and too broad to resolve. Upon returning to room temperature, only the small peak at 16.1 Å remains.

 The HTXRD scans for the $M_2(HT)_2$ are given in figure 6. In the initial scan of Cloisite® 20A there three peaks. The peak at 24.1 Å is interpreted to be the 001 reflection. The second and third peaks are at 16.1 Å and 12.2 Å respectively. At 200 °C there is only one peak present at 16.1 Å this peak is small but present at all temperatures. At 350 °C two separate peaks are clearly visible at 16.1 Å and at 13.4 Å. Heating after this point causes the 13.4 Å peak to shift further to the right to a value of 10.1 Å while broadening and disappearing at 750 °C. The final scan, upon cooling back to 25 °C, reveals only a single peak at 16.1 Å.

The HTXRD scans for $M(HT)_3$ are shown in figure 7. The initial scan for this organoclay indicates a 001 reflection at 34.1 Å; this peak tails off to the right. There is also a barely resolvable reflection at about 12.2 Å. When the organoclay reaches 350 °C there is only one peak present at 16.0 Å. This peak is again present for all the high temperature scans. At 450 °C another peak emerges at 14.1 Å. At 500 °C a much smaller peak begins to form at 10.1 Å. As heating continues, the peak at 16.0 Å remains unchanged, the 14.1 Å diminishes, and the peak at 10.1 Å becomes more defined. The final scan upon cooling back to 25 °C shows only the peak at 16.0 Å.

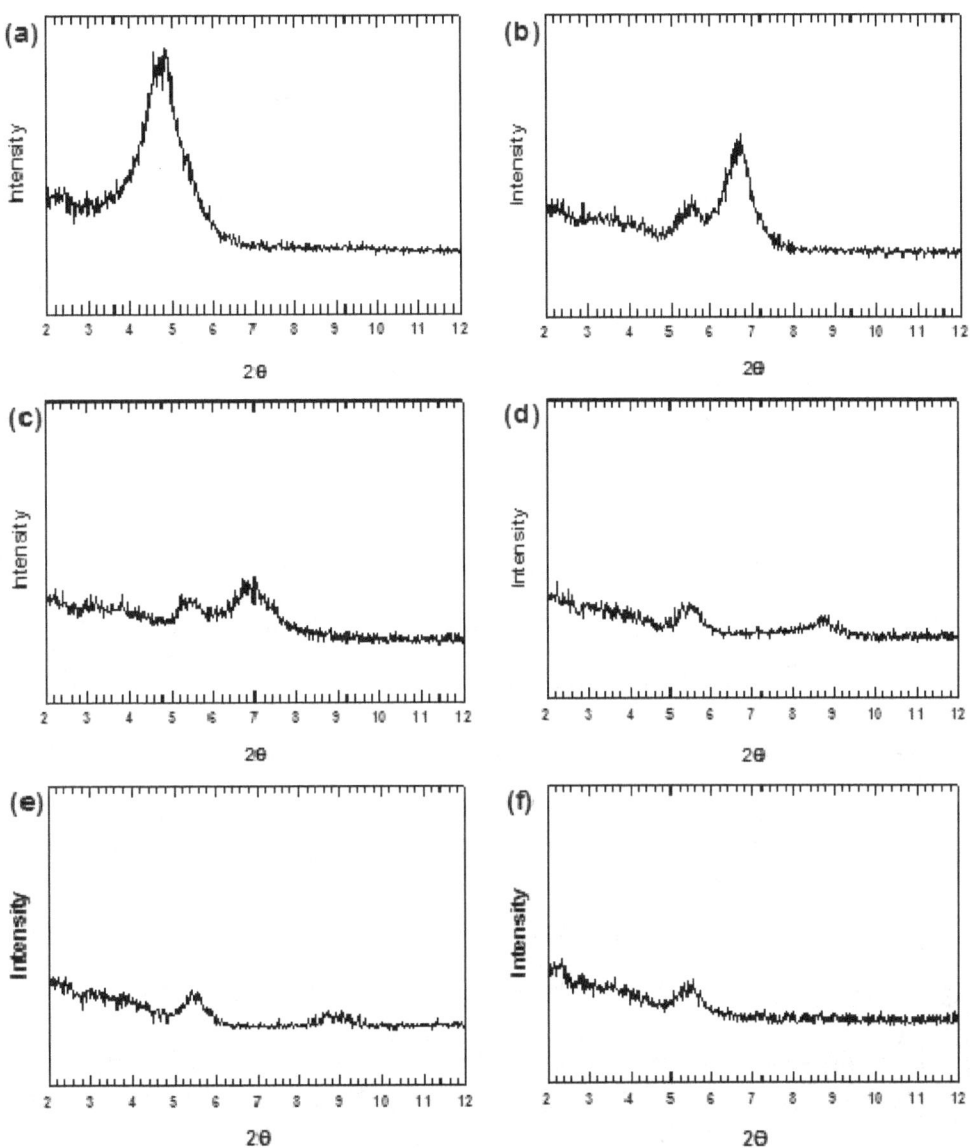

Figure 5: M$_3$(HT) HTXRD Data. (a) initial scan at 25 ^{o}C (b) 350 ^{o}C (c) 500 ^{o}C (d) 650 ^{o}C (e) 800 ^{o}C (f) final scan, cooled to 25 ^{o}C

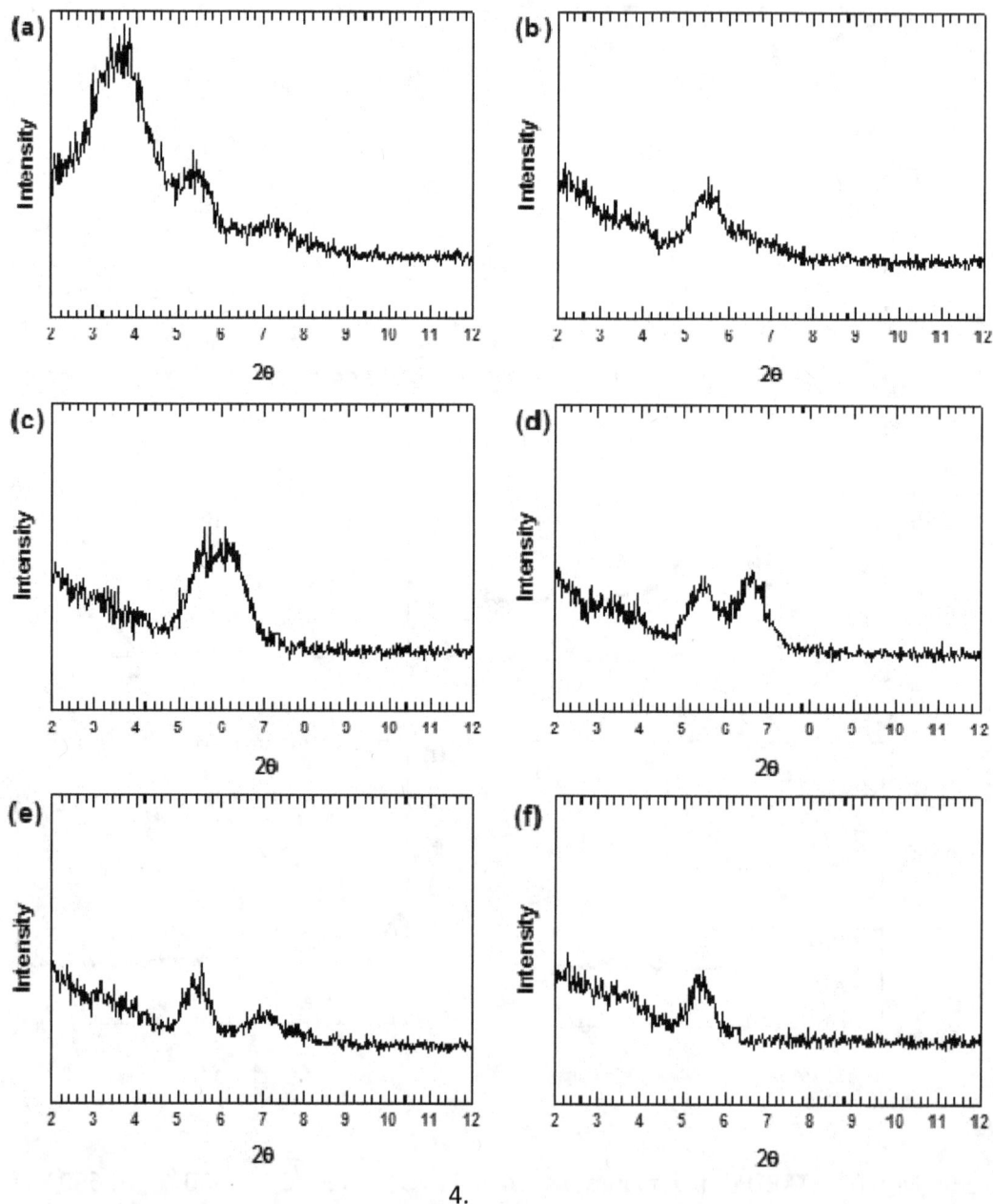

4.

Figure 6: Cloisite® 20A, (M$_2$(HT)$_2$) HTXRD Data. (a) Initial scan at 25 ^{o}C (b) 200 ^{o}C (c) 300 ^{o}C (d) 350 ^{o}C (e) 550 ^{o}C (f) Final scan, cooled to 25 ^{o}C

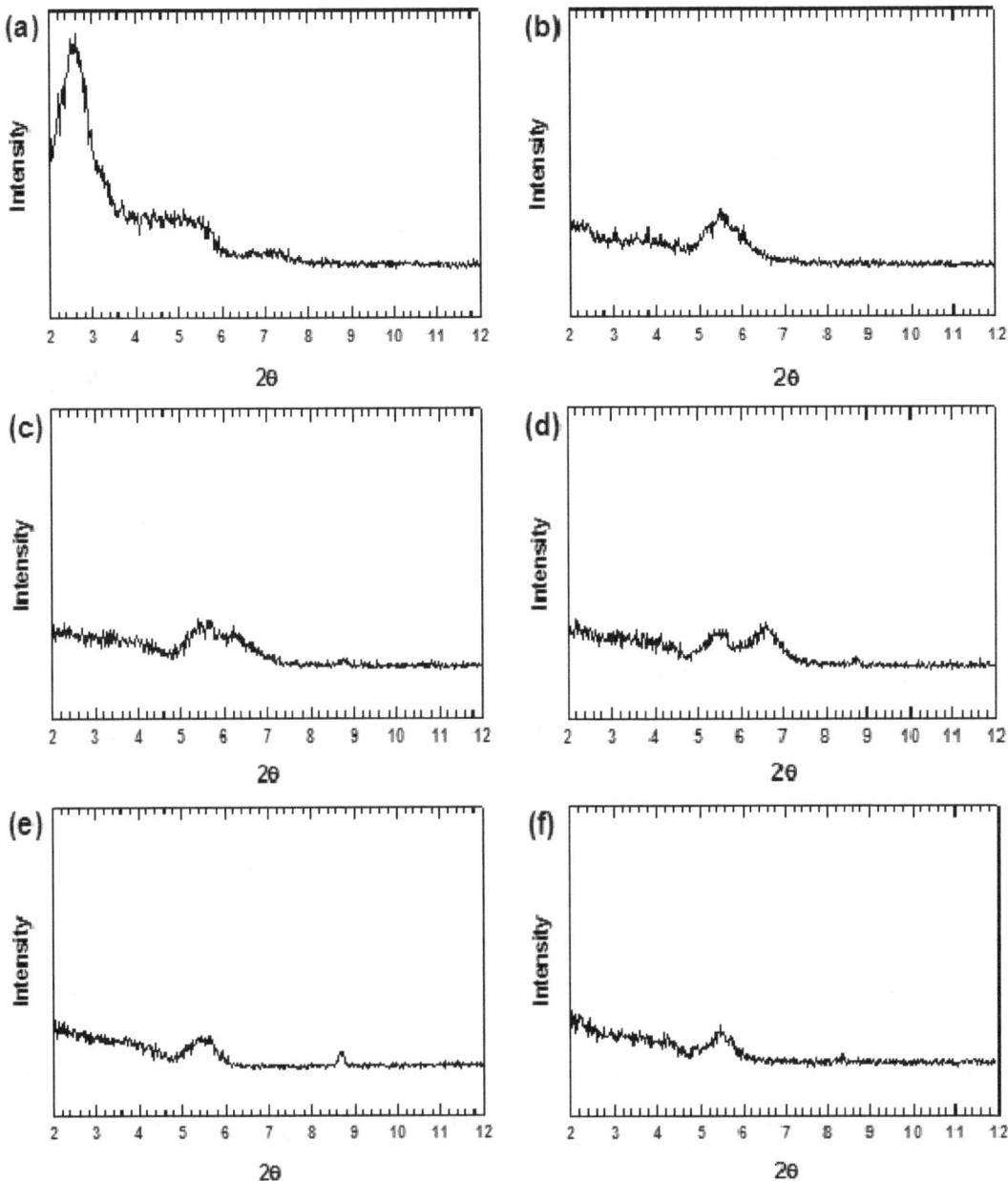

Figure 7: M(HT)₃ HTXRD Data. (a) Initial scan at 25 $^{\circ}$C (b) 350 $^{\circ}$C (c) 450 $^{\circ}$C (d) 500 $^{\circ}$C (e) 850 $^{\circ}$C (f) Final scan, cooled to 25 $^{\circ}$C.

17

Clearly surfactant structure does affect the process by which self-assembly happens, as comparison shows that the temperature response for these three organoclays is not uniform. By comparison:

1. All of the organoclays exhibit the 16.1 Å peak on final degradation. This is not the

    phase one would expect for the fully degraded organoclay, as MMT should display

    ~ 10Å d_{001} spacing.

2. At 350°C both the "one-tailed" and the "two-tailed" organoclays exhibit two phases

    or peaks at ~ 16Å and ~ 13Å. As temperature is increased in both cases, the ~ 13Å

    peak shifts to the right, becoming the expected ~ 10Å phase for fully collapsed MMT.

    However, the ~ 16Å phase remains present.

3. The "three tailed" organoclay does not appear to exhibit the two phases until 450°C

to 500°C.

It is interesting to compare these changes in nanostructure to information about chemical degradation of the organic content. When TGA is the "detector" for the onset of chemical degradation for aliphatic quaternary ammonium ions, a variety of onset temperatures are observed depending on whether the ammonium ion alone is tested, the organoclay, or a nanocomposite containing the organoclay. This can range from $180°C$ for the former case to temperatures more indicative of the degradation of the polymer ($300°C$ or more) in the latter case[5, 6]. In the absence of a polymer matrix, the degradation temperatures do increase with increasing number of tails in the surfactant, indicating that a "three-tailed" surfactant is the most stable. The TGA evidence for this is given in figures 8, 9 and 10. Comparison with the XRD information indicates that structural changes happen at temperatures above the TGA-based degradation temperature of the organoclay for all three organoclays. However, the order of stability seems to be supported, since the TGA-"stable" organoclay, the "three-tailed" material, exhibited a XRD structural change onset at a higher temperature than the other two.

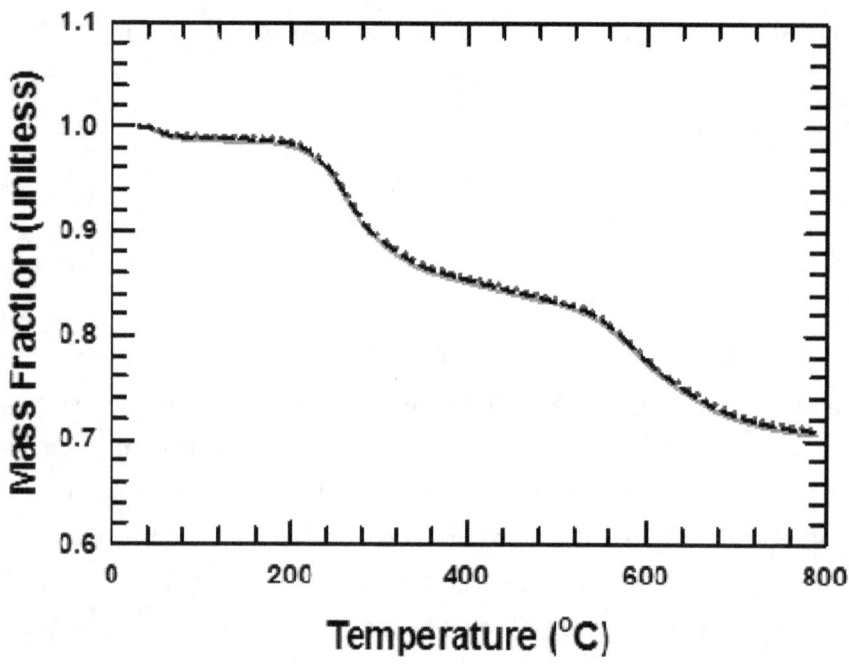

Figure 8: M$_3$(HT), "one-tailed" organoclay TGA data, 2 replicates. Mass fraction remaining = 0.71. Degradation onset = 200°C.

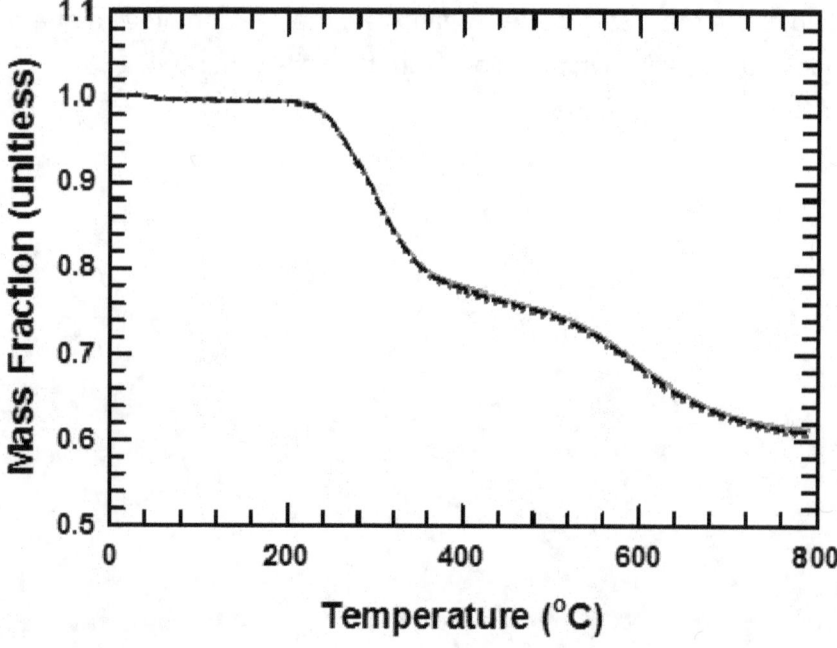

Figure 9: Cloisite 20A, M$_2$(HT)$_2$, "two-tailed" organoclay TGA data, 2 replicates. Mass fraction remaining = 0.61. Degradation onset = 205°C.

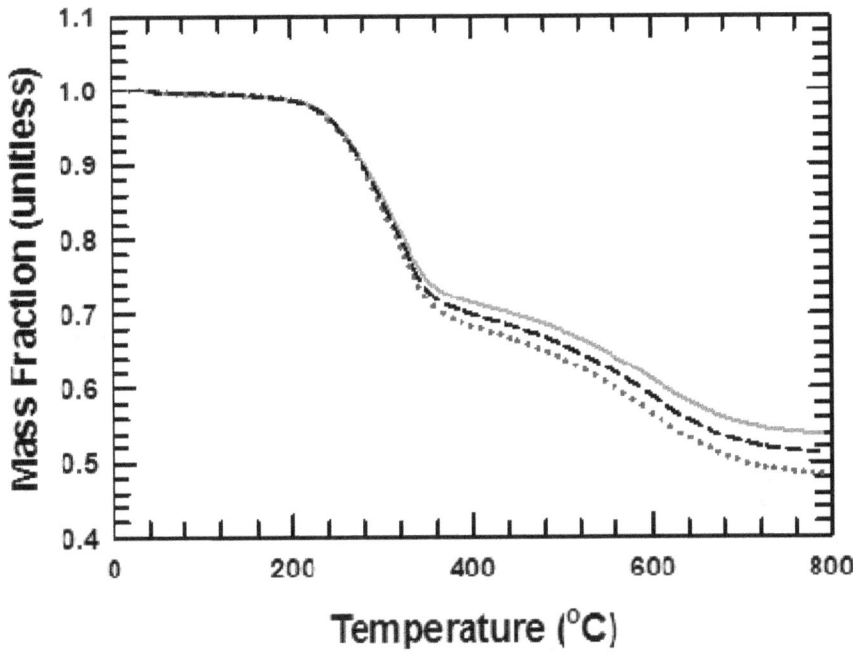

Figure 10: M(HT)$_3$ "three-tailed" organoclay TGA data, 2 replicates. The mass fraction remaining = 0.51. Degradation onset= 220°C.

A fourth organoclay was also characterized by HTXRD to attempt to benchmark our results to results published by Tang and Lewin [7]. These authors used a maleated polypropylene/organoclay composite annealed in 12.5% air in N$_2$ at various temperatures from 200°C to 300°C. They did transfer the material from an oven to the XRD. They showed a temperature dependence of interlayer distance, with the d$_{001}$ increasing from ~3 nm up to 4 nm with increasing temperature, and then formation of a phase at 1 nm upon further heating to 300°C. The organoclay utilized was Nanomer I.44P.

The results of our benchmark study are shown below, using the same Nanomer I.44P and maleated polypropylene as that used by Tang and Lewin (H. Stretz visited the laboratory at Polytechnical University and obtained these materials directly from Lewin.) The results do not match those reported by Tang and Lewin. In fact, as shown in figures 11 and 12, no change in the XRD scan was seen at all for either air or nitrogen environment. As the samples were not disturbed between the degradation step and the scan step in the current studies, an aerogel-type structure is assumed to be formed on undisturbed heating. Examples of montmorillonite clay aerogels have been reported by Bandi et al, and others.[8, 9] Clearly the organic portion in the barrier layer must have degraded, but as shown in the last section, degradation of the organic material as measured by TGA and changes in structure do not occur at the same temperature.

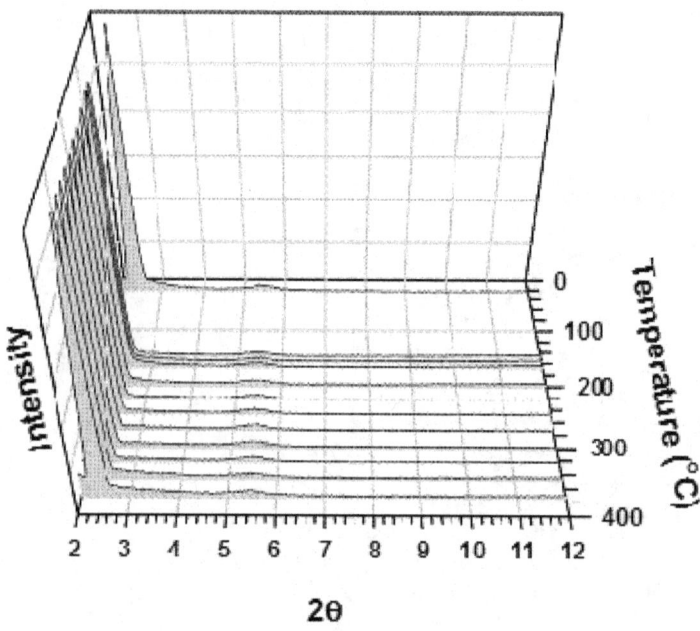

Figure 11: Polybond X5140/Nanomer I.44P 5% (w/w), heated in air.

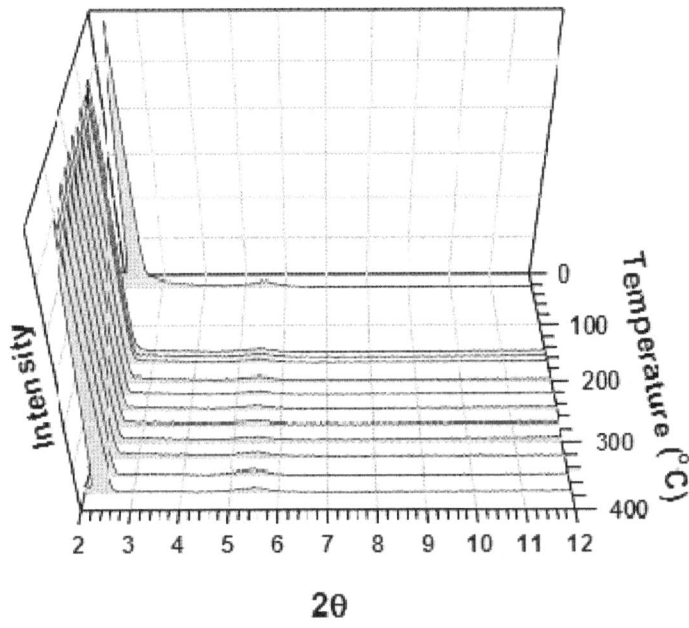

Figure 12: Polybond X5140/Nanomer I.44P 5% (w/w), heated in nitrogen.

The pristine organoclay was also submitted to this type of in-situ heating (stepped) followed by XRD analysis. The results are shown in figure 13 below. Even at very high temperatures, the organoclay shows no structural changes.

A comparison of the organic content of Nanomer I.44P to the Southern Clay materials by XRD is shown in figure 14 below. Paul et al. [10] have shown that the d_{001} can be predicted by the volume of the organic content in the organoclay. Experimental XRD d_{001} values from the current study for Southern Clay organoclays compare well with values as predicted by the published model. However, the Nanomer I.44P values do not fall on this predicted line, indicating some structural difference in the virgin (unheated) organoclays (compared to the Southern Clay materials). This difference might have led to the eventual production of an aerogel layer on heating.

To further explore the differences, the next section in this study discusses results of constant temperature, variable pressure experiments.

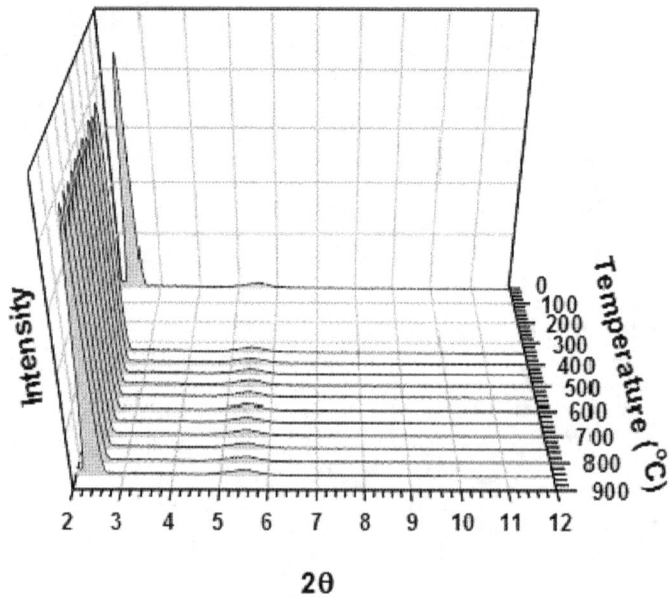

Figure 13: Nanomer I.44P Organoclay XRD analysis heated in air.

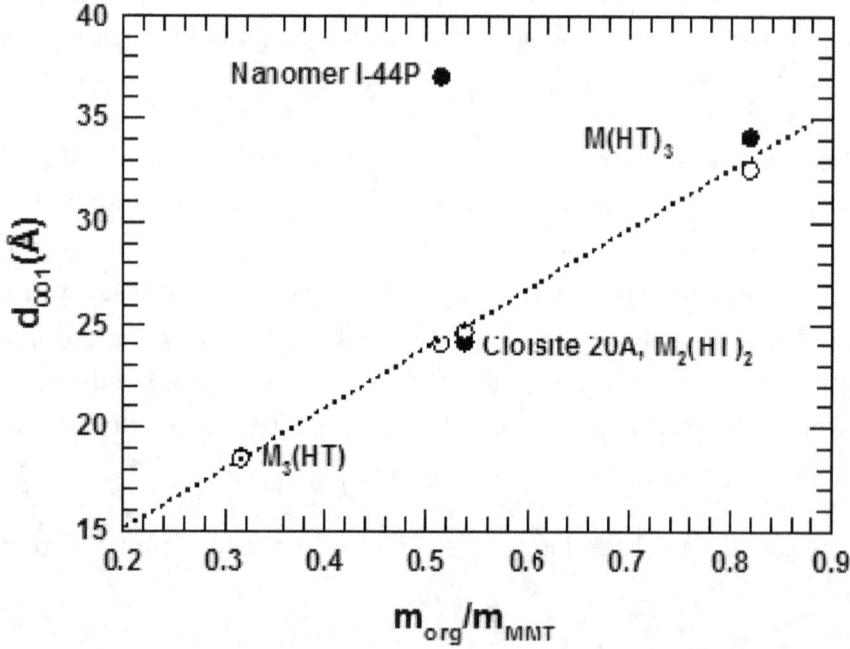

Figure 14: Comparison of experimental d_{001} to predicted d_{001}. Experimental data is solid, predictions are unfilled. Dotted line is a guide for the eye.

4.1. Effect of Processing Pressure on Evolution of Nanostructure in Organoclay at Fire Temperatures

Processing pressure has been postulated to be an important factor in the dispersion of organoclays during compounding. Given this information, researchers have postulated that the pressure at which materials were processed prior to XRD testing may have caused a difference in the XRD results seen by Tang and Lewin[7] versus results seen in figures 11 and 12. To test this hypothesis, the Cloisite 20A organoclay was first exposed to moderate pressure (~7 kPa) between the heated plates of a Carver press at typical polymer processing temperatures for a varying amount of time, and the evolution of the collapse of the layer spacing was documented by XRD (see figure 15). This study is also a benchmark, as a similar study has been reported by Yoon et al.[11]

These scans are shifted vertically for clarity. The unpressed sample has a peak for the 001 reflection at 24.9 Å and a smaller peak at 12.1 Å which is interpreted as the d_{002}. Pressing the sample for one minute yielded a less intense 001 reflection, which was shifted slightly to 25.9 Å. The second peak is also shifted slightly to 12.7 Å. The scan for material pressed for five minutes reveals that both peaks are shifted even further to 29.3 Å and 13.5 Å, respectively. The 001 reflection becomes less intense, while the second peak begins to increase in intensity. The sample that was pressed for ten minutes also has two peaks present: the 001 reflection at 37.2 Å and a second peak now at 14.0 Å. These peaks continue the trend that is shown in the previous samples.

Since the XRD behavior at high temperature was different for Cloisite 20A and Nanomer I44.P, the shift in phase behavior with pressure seen for Cloisite 20A can be compared at these low temperatures to that seen for the Nanomer material in figure 16. Note that under pressure, the Nanomer organoclay behaves the same essentially as Cloisite 20A. The d_{001} in the unmagnified scan is at 36.9 Å. The smaller peak is at 16.1 Å. After pressing, a new phase is formed with a characteristic d-spacing of 13.8 Å, and the intercalated phase has disappeared. Thus if both pressure and heat are applied simultaneously, even at low temperatures, the Nanomer clay particle structure collapses just as Cloisite 20A did in the absence of pressure. It is concluded that even very moderate pressure is an important factor in the development of barrier layer structure. We have only identified one organoclay which apparently is responsive to pressure, Nanomer I44.P. The difference between the virgin Nanomer organoclay and the other three organoclays tested is likely related to the surfactant.

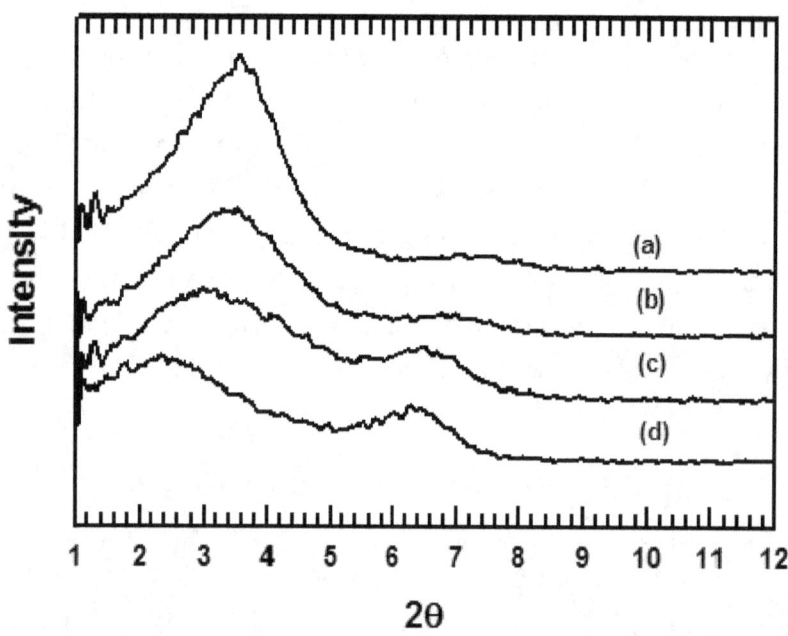

Figure 15: XRD scans of pressed (~7kPa, 250°C) Cloisite 20A: (a) unpressed (b) 1 min (c) 5 min (d) 10 min.

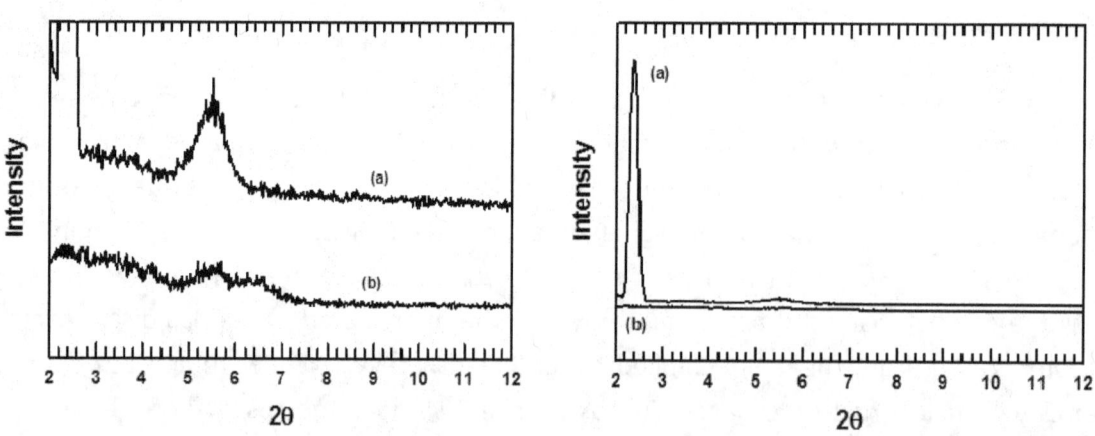

Figure 16: XRD scans of pressed Nanomer I44.P organoclay: (a)unpressed (b) pressed. Scan on left is magnified version.

To extend this work, we have obtained TEM photomicrographs of the Cloisite 20A, which showed a change in structure before and after pressing. These are presented in figures 17 and 18.

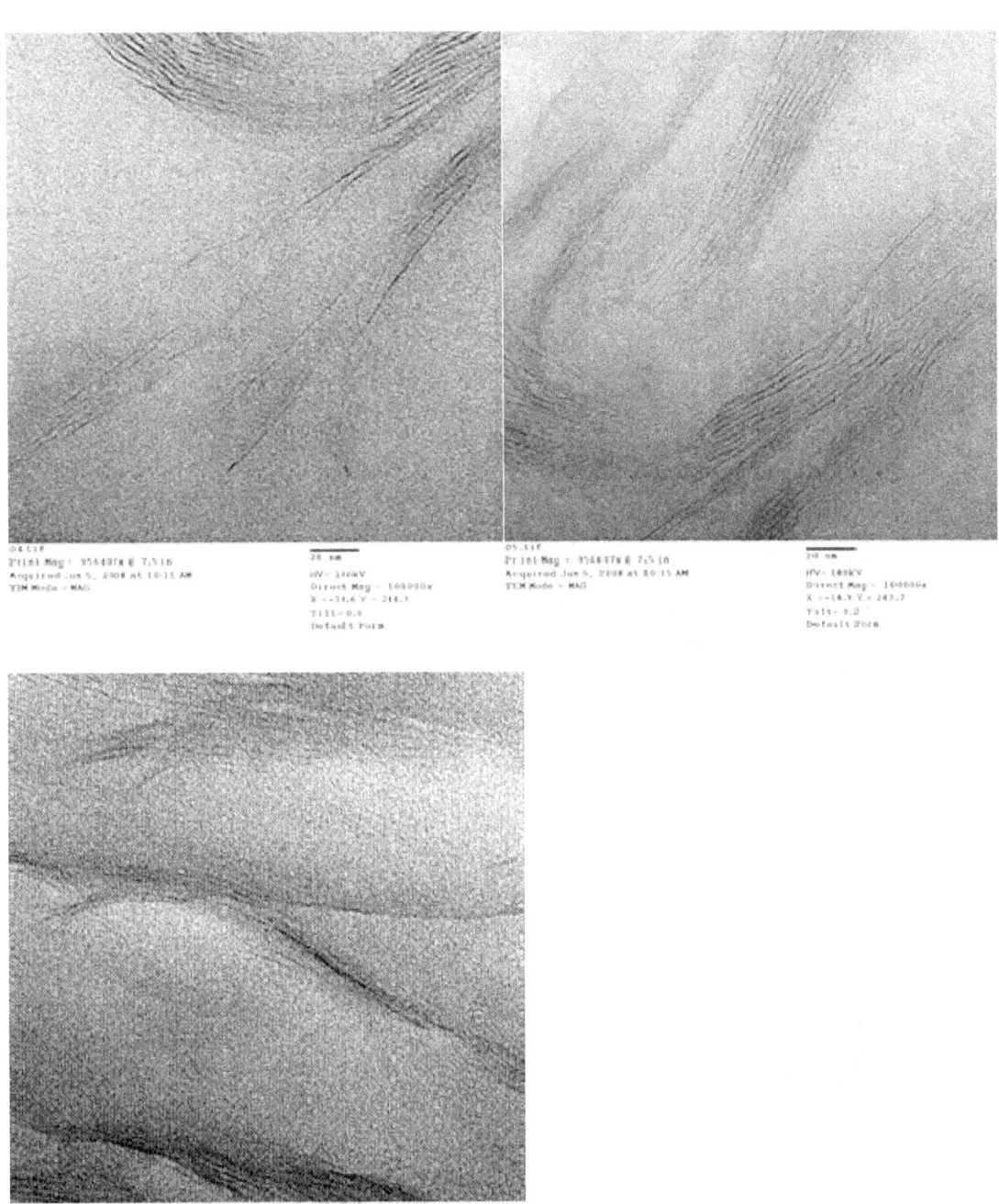

Figure 17: Multiple TEM images of unpressed Cloisite 20A.

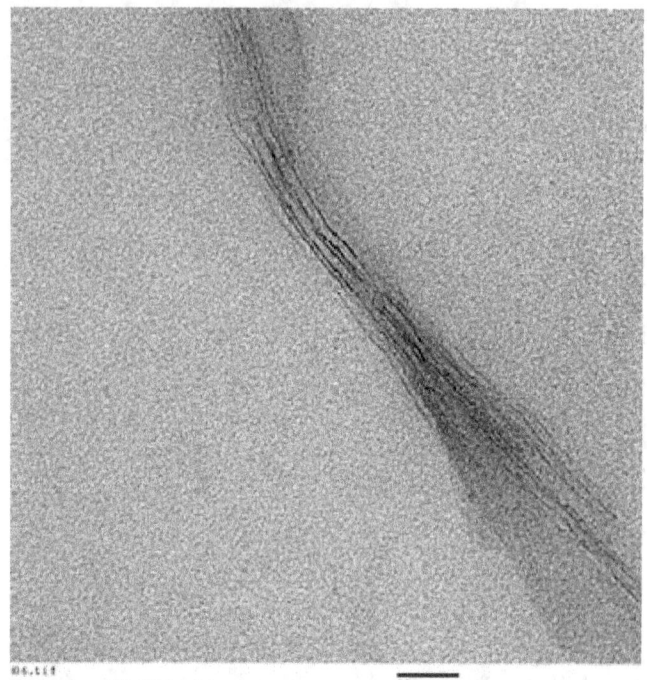

04.tif
Print Mag = 956407x @ 7.5 in
Acquired Jun 23, 2008 at 11:46 AM
TEM Mode = MAG

20 nm
HV = 180kV
Direct Mag = 100000x
X = 28.2 Y = 125.5
Tilt = 0.0
Default Form

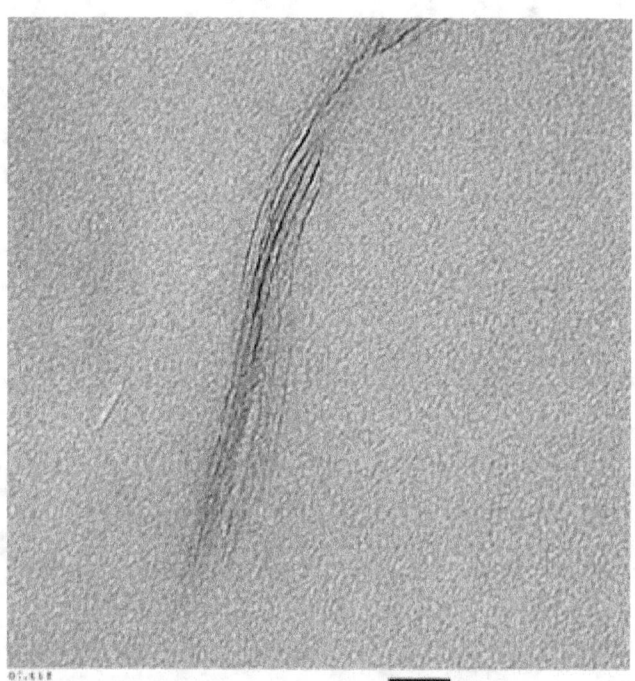

05.tif
Print Mag = 956407x @ 7.5 in
Acquired Jun 23, 2008 at 11:49 AM
TEM Mode = MAG

20 nm
HV = 180kV
Direct Mag = 100000x
X = 17.3 Y = 126.5
Tilt = 0.0
Default Form

Figure 18: TEM image of pressed Cloisite 20A.

Clearly the XRD showed another phase being formed during pressing, but no gross changes can be observed in the TEM images. A very interesting "fine-scale" phenomenon can be noted, however, in the top photomicrograph in figure 18. Here a hybrid type of stacking occurs, with alternating distances between the plates. While we do not have enough TEM data yet to corroborate; changes in the XRD and this change in the TEM appear to be correlated, and the effect presents an intriguing possibility for future studies. A diagram of this effect is shown in figure 19. Note that these regularly alternating interlayers have been reported in synthetic fluorohectorites as early as 1996 by Pinnavaia et al.[12-15] In graphite alternating structures such as this are referred to as "**staged heterostructures**."

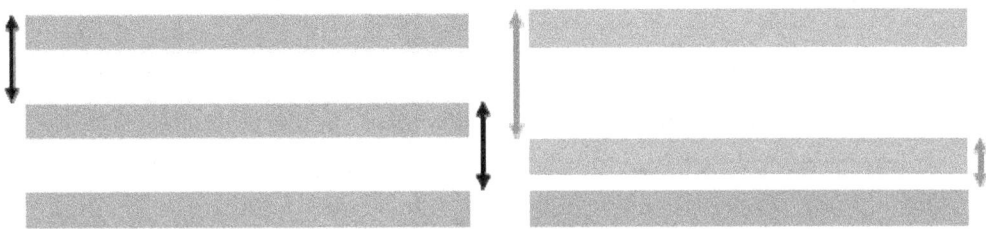

Figure 19: Diagram showing possible structural effects of bulk pressure. (a) Equal d-spacing between MMT platelets in stack before and (b) unequal d-spacing afterwards.

The observations related to surfactant structure are summarized in Table II below.

Table II: Summary of XRD Results

Organoclay	Surfactant Structure	Experimental Conditions	Does the organoclay show a collapse in d_{001}?
Nanomer® I-44P	dimethyl, bis-di(hydrogenated tallow) ammonium (two-tailed)*	unpressed, composite in air, composite in N_2	no
	---	pressed	yes
M_3(HT)	trimethyl hydrogenated tallow ammonium (one-tailed)	unpressed	yes
Cloisite® 20A, M_2(HT)$_2$	dimethyl, bis-di(hydrogenated tallow) ammonium (two-tailed)	unpressed, pressed, TEM	yes

M(HT)$_3$	methyl, tri(hydorgenated tallow) ammonium (three-tailed)	unpressed	yes

4.2. Permeability: A Novel Test Method for Following Evolution of Nanostructure of Degraded Organoclays

The reason for the permeability studies was to develop an alternative analytical technique to corroborate XRD information. Here we use permeability of the organoclay ash as a bulk-scale property to detect micron-scale structural changes in the stacking of MMT platelets. **This novel method provides us with a multi-scale approach for analyzing the structure of the barrier layer upon degradation**, relating a bulk property (permeability) to a nanoscale property (XRD response).

The composite models will predict how structural changes on the micron scale relate to permeability changes on the bulk scale. These models also allow a guide for better interpretation of the experimental results. In this section three types of information are presented. First, the models are reviewed. Second the model predictions for relative permeabilities are compared to actual relative mass loss rates. The experimental values used were taken from the literature and represented a typical polyolefin based nanocomposite. By comparing theoretical transport rates to actual, we address the question:

"can restriction of the flow of gases be responsible for the reduced mass loss rate seen in nanocomposite flammability tests?"

Finally experimental determinations of the steady state mass flux for MMT clay and ash are presented. These fluxes are then compared to answer a second question:

"is permeability a technique which is sensitive to micron-scale structural change?"

4.2.1. Overview of composite models for permeability

Various models for composite permeability as they relate to nanocomposites have been reviewed recently by Paul and Robeson[16].

The simplest way to model any composite property is to use a rule of mixtures approach. Polymer nanocomposite properties, however, do not generally follow this rule. Instead, fillers with high aspect ratio particles will influence the permeability of gases through the matrix more than filler particles with lower aspect ratios. Alignment/orientation of the filler particles (with respect to the axis of gas permeation) also plays a significant role in bulk permeability. Five models are briefly described in the following section. Predictions from these models are later compared to experimental mass loss rates.

4.2.1.1.   Nielsen Model: This model describes the maximum decrease in permeability that can be expected for the addition of a filler material to a polymer based on tortuosity arguments alone. There are a few key assumptions in this model. The particles in this model are assumed to be impermeable, which results in the diffusing molecules having to go around the filler particles. Conceptually the molecules have a longer, more tortuous path to travel, thus resulting in a longer time required for diffusion across the membrane. This idea is illustrated in figure 20.

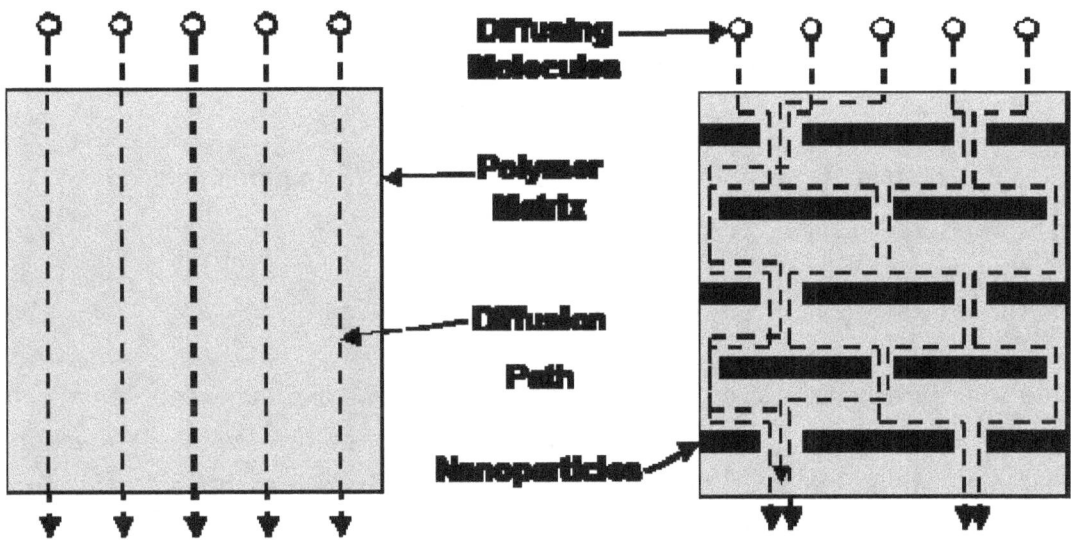

Figure 20: Illustration of gas molecule path through a virgin matrix (left) versus a composite (right).

The filler is assumed to be of the same size uniformly and completely dispersed in the composite matrix parallel to the surface of the composite. Finally, the matrix properties are not affected by the presence of filler. Incomplete dispersion, voids, and non parallel alignment of particles would result in higher permeabilities than predicted by this model. The relative permeability is given as:

$$\frac{P}{P_0} = \frac{1-\phi}{1+\alpha\phi/2}$$ (1)

where P is the permeability of the composite, P_0 is the permeability of the neat polymer, φ is the volume fraction of the filler, and α is the aspect ratio of the filler particles given by equation (2).

$$\alpha = \frac{w}{t} \tag{2}$$

Here w is the intermediate dimension of the particle and t is the smallest dimension of the particle.[17]

4.2.1.2.   Bharadwaj Model - Like the Nielsen model, the Bharadwaj model is based strictly on tortuosity arguments. The main difference is the consideration of the orientation and alignment of the particles. Where the Nielsen model assumed that the particles were perfectly aligned perpendicular to the gas flow, the Bharadwaj model makes no such assumption. The Bharadwaj model for the relative permeability of a composite is given by equation (3),

$$\frac{P}{P_0} = \frac{1-\phi}{1 + \frac{\alpha\phi}{2}\left(\frac{2}{3}\right)\left(S + \frac{1}{2}\right)} \tag{3}$$

where P, P_0, φ, and α retain the previous definitions, and S is the order parameter given by equation (4),

$$S = \frac{1}{2}\left\langle 3\cos^2\theta - 1\right\rangle \tag{4}$$

where θ is the angle between the direction of preferred orientation and the sheet normal unit vectors. The brackets represent an average over the entire set of particles within the system. The order parameter ranges in value from –½ to 1. A value of –½ represents an orthogonal orientation for the particles in the composite. A value of 1 indicates a perfect alignment of the particles perpendicular to the gas flow. This value of S causes the model to collapse to the Nielsen model. A value of 0 for the order parameter indicates a random orientation.[18]   A diagram of the meaning of the orientation factor is given in figure 21.

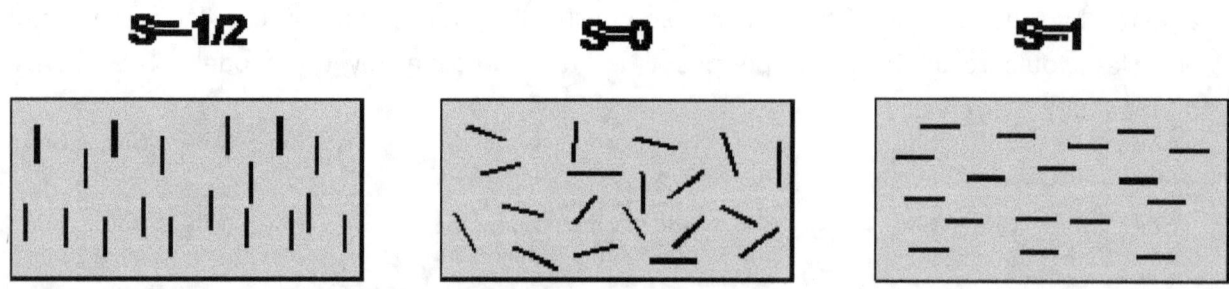

Figure 21: Orientation of particles corresponding to orientation factor, S.

4.2.1.3.   <u>Fredrickson and Bicerano Model</u> - In this model the filler particles are disk shaped, whereas in the previous two models the particles are assumed to be ribbon-like. These plate-like particles are impermeable with net orientation of the plates, but there is not positional order for the plates, which creates a nematic phase. This model focuses on dilute and semi-dilute regimes (i.e. the volume fraction of particles is small). It is assumed that the permeability of the polymer is not influenced by the presence of particles in the matrix. The final equation given by Fredrickson and Bicerano is equation (5),

$$\frac{P}{P_0} = \frac{1}{4}\left(\frac{1}{1+a_1\kappa\alpha\phi} + \frac{1}{1+a_2\kappa\alpha\phi}\right)^2 \tag{5}$$

where P, P_0, φ, and α retain their previous definitions, and κ is a geometric factor. In this case the aspect ratio is the ratio of radial dimension of the disk to the thickness. The geometric factor, κ, for this model is given by equation(6).

$$\kappa = \frac{\pi}{\ln\alpha} \tag{6}$$

The values for a_1 and a_2 are [2-sqrt (2)]/4 and [2+sqrt (2)]/4, respectively. (See Fredrickson and Bicerano for details.) [19]

4.2.1.4.   Cussler Model - All of the assumptions from the Nielsen model remain in the Cussler model except for the regularity of the array. The Cussler Model for relative permeability of a composite with monodisperse particles in a regular array is given by equation (7)

$$\frac{P}{P_0} = \frac{1-\phi}{1-\phi+\alpha^2\phi^2} \tag{7}$$

where α is the aspect ratio of the particle given by equation (8),

$$\alpha = \frac{R}{t} \tag{8}$$

and R is ½ the intermediate dimension of the filler particle and t is the smallest dimension of the filler particle. The Cussler model for relative permeability of a composite with monodisperse particles in a <u>random</u> array is given below.[20]

$$\frac{P}{P_0} = \frac{1-\phi}{\left(1+\frac{2}{3}\alpha\phi\right)^2} \tag{9}$$

4.2.1.5.   Gusev and Lusti Model - The Gusev and Lusti model is derived from a computer simulation. This allows more variables to be taken into account than the previous models. This model accounts for the geometric factors associated with the increased tortuosity as well as the changes in the permeability of the polymer matrix on the molecular level. The Gusev and Lusti model for the relative permeability of a composite is given in equation (10),

$$\frac{P}{P_0} = \exp\left[-\left(\frac{\alpha\phi}{x_0}\right)^{\beta}\right]$$
(10)

where x_0 and β are constants determined by a regression on computer generated data. The values given by Gusev and Lusti for the constants are $\beta=0.71$ and $x_0=3.47$.[21]

4.2.2. Comparison of model permeability predictions to relative mass loss rate

The current theories for the flammability reduction describe a barrier layer that forms on the surface of the degraded nanocomposite [2-4, 7, 22]. This layer is composed of aligned, high aspect ratio, impermeable platelets and acts as an obstacle to the transfer of heat and mass between the bulk polymer and its environment. In order to confirm this theory, experimental data for the relative peak mass loss rate (RPMLR) of a polymer nanocomposite will be compared to that of the relative permeability of the nanocomposite. If these two numbers are similar in scale this should indicate that tortuous path arguments are a potential contribution to the often noted reduction in mass loss rate (MLR). It should be noted that these calculations are based on the contribution of only the filler particles, and do not account for the influence of char formation.

The data that will be used for this comparison comes from Gilman et al.[23] This work contains data for the peak MLR of neat polypropylene (PP) and polypropylene/montmorillonite (PP/MMT) nanocomposites. The two PP/MT composites in this work contain 2 percent and 4 percent by weight of filler. The RPMLR is calculated by dividing the peak MLR of the composite material by the peak MLR of the neat polymer. The comparison of the RPMLR to the relative permeabilities calculated by the models is shown in table III (all relative permeabilities were calculated using an aspect ratio of $\alpha=50$ [24].) The model that most closely predicts the observed RPMLR is the Cussler model [20] (with a random array) for both volume fractions of filler examined.

Upon examination of the data in Table III, clearly the predicted relative permeability is always greater than the experimentally observed RPMLR (note for 2% (v/v) MMT, the experimental value is 0.34). However, the predicted values are always of the same magnitude as the experimental ones. This observation is a necessary though insufficient proof that the permeability and the mass loss rate are related, supporting the theories that mass transport limitations are responsible for the flammability reduction of a nanocomposite material.

Table III- Predicted Relative Permeabilities

		$\phi = 0.02$	$\phi = 0.04$
Observed Relative Peak Mass Loss Rate* (RPMLR)		0.34	0.28
Neilsen Model		0.65	0.48
Bharadwaj Model			
	+S= -1/2	0.98	0.96
	S = 0	0.84	0.72
	S = 1	0.65	0.48
Fredrickson and Bicerano Model		0.67	0.50
Cussler Model			
	Monodisperse	0.55	0.35
	Polydisperse	0.80	0.49
Gusev and Lusti Model		0.66	0.51

* Calculated from data given by Gilman et al.[23]

+ S refers to filler orientation

4.2.3. Sensitivity of experimental flux of Ar to micron-scale structural change in organoclay ash

Currently there is no data available for the permeability of MMT clay or its degraded ash when it forms a barrier layer. This permeability is determined in this work through the use of a diffusion apparatus. The details of the experimental setup and procedure were given earlier. Note that the formed ash membranes are mechanically fragile, and, as a result, the ash was sandwiched between two highly permeable layers consisting of track etched polycarbonate (TEPC) membranes with 0.03 μm holes to give it structural stability in the diffusion apparatus and allow the edges of the sample to seal. The high permeability of these membranes allows the permeability of the MMT to be seen without significant resistance from the membranes themselves. The diffusing gas in these experiments was argon for convenience, though fluxes of other gases more representative of degrading polymers is planned for future tests. The data that was obtained from these experiments is presented in figure 22. The plateau concentrations in figure 22 can be used to calculate steady state fluxes, as the plateau represents a steady state condition in which gas is moving through the ash or organoclay at a constant rate. The molar flux of Ar, J^*_{Ar}, was calculated using equation (11).

$$J^*_{Ar} = \frac{c_{Ar} \cdot V_{N_2}}{A}$$
(11)

Here c_{Ar} is the molar concentration of Argon on the sample side, V_{N2} is the volumetric flowrate of the carrier gas, and A is the cross-sectional area of the membrane. The relevant fluxes corresponding to data in figure 22 are given in Table IV. The mass fluxes, j_{Ar}, in this table are calculated by multiplying the molar fluxes by the molecular mass of argon. Note that in this particular experimental setup, a concentration gradient is driving diffusion, not a pressure gradient. This corresponds to the case found in a burning polymer sample, in which the gas produced inside the nanocomposite is at atmospheric pressure, the backside of the sample is at atmospheric pressure, and the flux of volatile organics towards the fire is driven by concentration.

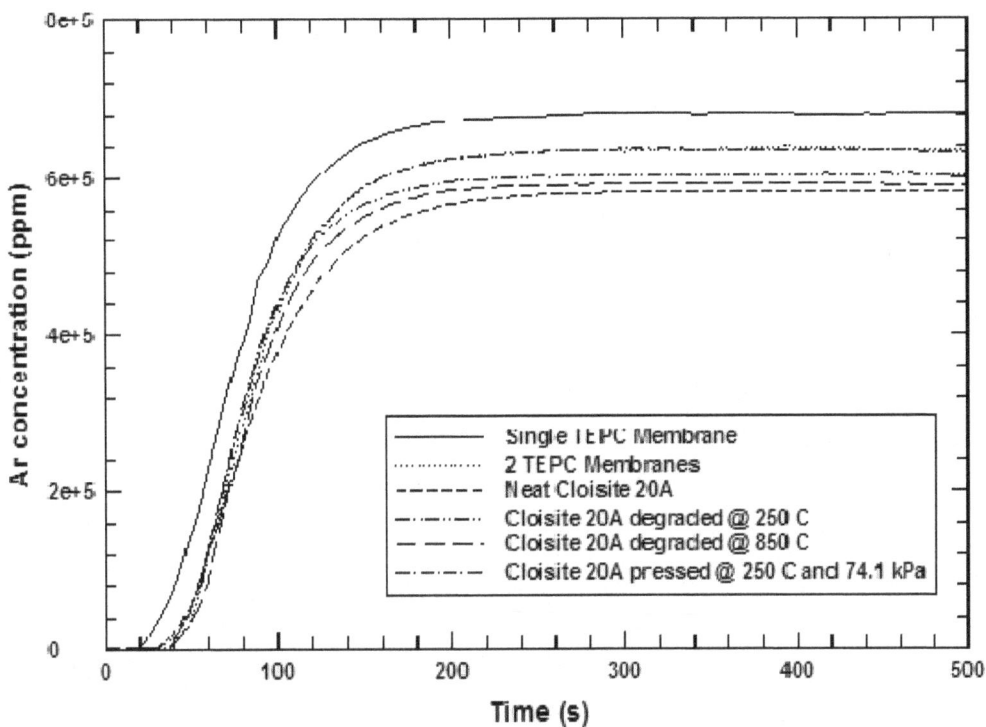

Figure 22: Permeability of Ar gas through Cloisite 20A Organoclay, pristine and ashed samples. For structural integrity, the organoclay/ash was sandwiched between two polycarbonate track etched membranes (TEPC).

Table IV - Fluxes Calculated from Permeability Data

Experiment	Membrane	c_{Ar} (mol/L)	J^*_{Ar} [mol/(m^2-s)]	j_{Ar} [g/(m^2-s)]
A	TEPC single	0.0279	0.162	6.49
B	TEPC double	0.0260	0.152	6.06
C	Cloisite 20A (unpressed)	0.0238	0.139	5.54
D	Cloisite 20A (heated to 250 °C in air, 15 min)	0.0247	0.144	5.74
E	Cloisite 20A (heated to 850 °C in air, 15 min)	0.0240	0.140	5.59
F	Cloisite 20A (pressed at 250 °C 74.1 kPa, 10 min)	0.0259	0.151	6.03

*Area for all membranes is 9.78 x 10^{-4} m^2, and carrier gas flowrate on the sample side was 9.5 sccm. The purge side was 30 sccm of pure Ar.

The baseline flux in Table IV is 0.162 mol/m^2-sec for a single TEPC membrane with a thickness of approximately 0.01 mm. For two TEPC membranes, this values is reduced to 0.152 mol/m^2-sec. This data is consistent with theory; the flux should go down as the thickness of the sample goes up.

In the next experiment, Cloisite 20A organoclay was formed into a monolith using a handheld apparatus consisting of an aluminum ring and a matching ram. The monolith was then deposited between two TEPC membranes and installed in the permeability chamber. Thus the Ar must transport through two layers of TEPC and one layer of Cloisite 20A of approximately 0.4 mm thickness. Given the additional resistance offered by the Cloisite 20A, the flux should go down from experiment B to experiment C, and it does.

In experiment D, the Cloisite 20A has now been degraded by heating to 250 °C. The flux goes up by a small value, perhaps indicating a structural change. If indeed there was degradation of the organic material in the organoclay, which is expected at that temperature, there would likely be void spaces produced during degradation. An increased flux is consistent with this idea.

In experiment E, the Cloisite 20A was degraded by heating at 850 °C, and the flux is nearly what it was in the case of the unheated organoclay. These small changes in flux may in fact represent only the reproducibility for this technique. Experiments C, D, and E, in fact, all exhibit the same permeability given this definition of reproducibility.

In experiment F, where the Cloisite 20A was pressed during heating, the flux is considerably higher than any of the previous three values. This cannot be explained by the expected increase in density of a compacted sample. The flux changes can; however, be explained by structural changes such as lowering of the filler particle aspect ratio.

5. Conclusions

The work described here was the result of a collaboration between researchers at Tennessee Technological University (H. A. Stretz, J. B. Fox) and Oak Ridge National Lab (A. Payzant, R. Meisner). The materials tested were primarily virgin organoclays. Researchers have explored: the effect of surfactant on barrier layer structural formation by high temperature in-situ x-ray diffractometry (HTXRD) as well as corroborating characterizations, the effect of pressure on barrier layer structure formation, and the use of permeability as a bulk scale technique for detecting structural changes in barrier layers of MMT.

Regarding the effects of surfactant, the following conclusions were reached.

a. All organoclays up to 800°C exhibited a 16Å phase, which is not the d_{001}

   expected of a fully degraded MMT (e.g. ~ 10Å).

b. All organoclays exhibited a "collapsed/collapsing" phase, ranging in d_{001} from

   13Å to 10Å, whose spacing depended on temperature.

c. Thermal stability of the surfactant (TGA) correlated with the onset of development of the "collapsing" phase identified in 1.b (XRD). Both M_3HT and

$M_2(HT)_2$ showed onset of this phase at ~350°C, while for $M_3(HT)$ onset appeared at 450-500°C.

d. Chemical changes (TGA) appear to occur at lower temperature than structural changes (XRD).

e. Differences were seen for a plot of m_{org}/m_{MMT} versus d_{001} for Nanomer-I.44P versus Cloisite 20A ($M_2(HT)_2$). These differences correlate to differences in structural stability. Nanomer I44.P appears structurally stable up to 800°C, suggesting production of an aerogel on heating.

Regarding the effects of pressure, the following conclusions were noted.

a. Cloisite 20A and Nanomer I44.P structural changes were compared by XRD at two conditions: high temperature (800°C) and room pressure versus low temperature (250°C) and 7 kPa of pressure. In the absence of pressure Nanomer I44.P appeared to produce an aerogel, while Cloisite 20A did not. Under pressure, however, both organoclays produced the same collapsed phase.

b. TEM images of the collapsed phase in Cloisite 20A show an interesting trend towards formation of "twins" within the stacks.

Regarding the significance of permeability as a bulk scale test for micron-scale changes in barrier layer structure, the following aspects were studied.

a. For five theoretical models examined, relative permeability predictions were always greater than experimentally observed relative peak mass loss rate (RPMLR).

b. The Cussler model with random arrays was closest predictor of experimental RPMLR.

c. Predicted values of permeability were of the same magnitude as RPMLR, supporting mass transport limitation theories for nanocomposite reduction in flammability.

d. Fluxes of Ar through 0.4 mm thickness of organoclay ash averaged 0.140 $mol/m^2 \cdot sec$.

e. Structural changes of heated/pressed Cloisite 20A as verified by XRD correlate to an increase in permeability of Ar through the ash. This data is not consistent with compaction of void spaces in the ash, but is consistent with structural change leading to lower filler particle aspect ratio.

2. Future Plans

a. A multidisciplinary team composed of a ceramic/aggregate sintering expert (J. Biernacki) and a nanocomposite fire performance expert (H. Stretz) will study the deformation of the ash. This team seeks analogs from aggregate sintering chemistry/physics which will lead to new in-situ formation of barrier layers with higher mechanical strength.

   b. Future XRD studies will be enabled by the planned purchase of a P'Analytical XRD Diffractometer at TTU, installation by summer 2009.

6. Acknowledgements

We gratefully acknowledge major support by the NIST Fire Research Division under grant 70NANB7H6006. Additional financial support was provided by the Center for Energy Systems Research at TTU and access to permeability apparatus was arranged courtesy of Dr. Joe Biernacki and Pravin Kannan at TTU.

Part of this research was sponsored through the Oak Ridge High Temperature Materials Laboratory User Program by the Assistant Secretary for Energy Efficiency and Renewable Energy, Office of FreedomCAR and Vehicle Technologies. This program, at Oak Ridge National Laboratory (ORNL), managed by UT-Batelle, LLC, is managed for the U. S. Department of Energy under contract number DE-AC05-00OR22725. Collaborators at ORNL included Dr. Andrew Payzant and Dr. Roberta Meisner, both crystallographers, who aided us with X-ray diffraction results.

In addition we gratefully acknowledge collaborative visits, discussions, and shared materials from Dr. Menachem Lewin at New York Polytechnic University. Equistar polypropylenes were provided by Mr. Tim Skillman.

The TEM images presented herein were prepared by Dr. Jibao He at Tulane University.

7. References

[1]   Gilman JW, Kashiwagi T, Morgan AB, Harris RH, Brassell L, Van Landingham M, Jackson CL. Flammmability of polymer clay nanocomposites consortium: year one annual report. Gaithersburg, MD: National Institute of Standards and Technology, 2000.

[2]   Kashiwagi T, Harris RHJ, Zhang X, Briber RM, Cipriano BH, Raghavan S, Awad WH, Shields JR. Polymer 2004;45:881.

[3]   Gilman JW, Harris RH, Shields JR, Kashiwagi T, Morgan AB. Polymers in Advanced Technologies 2006;17:263-271.

[4]   Lewin M. Polymers for Advanced Technologies 2006;17:758-763.

[5]   Leszczynska A, Njuguna J, Pielichowski K, Banerjee JR. Thermochimica Acta 2007;453(2):75-96.

[6]   Suter UW, Osman MA, Ploetze M. Journal of Materials Chemistry 2003;13:2359.

[7]   Tang Y, Lewin M. Polymer Degradation and Stability 2007;92:53-60.

[8]   Bandi S, Bell M, Schiraldi DA. Macromolecules 2005;38:9216-9220.

[9]   Somlai LS, Bandi S, Schiraldi DA, Mathias LJ. AIChE Journal 2006;52(3):1162-1168.

[10]   Paul DR, Zeng QH, Yu AB, Lu GQ. Chemistry of Materials 2005;17:In press.

[11]   Yoon PJ, Paul DR, Hunter DL. Polymer 2003(44):5323.

[12]   Ijdo WL, Pinnavaia TJ. Journal of Solid State Chemistry 1998;139:281-289.

[13]   Ijdo WL, Pinnavaia TJ. Chemistry of Materials 1999;11:3227-3231.

[14]   Ijdo WL, Pinnavaia TJ. Green Chemistry 2001;3:10-12.

[15]   Ijdo WL, Lee T, Pinnavaia TJ. Advanced Materials 1996;8(1):79-83.

[16]   Paul DR, Robeson LM. Polymer 2008;49:3187-3204.

[17]   Nielsen LE. Journal of Macromolecular Science 1967;A1 (5):929-942.

[18]   Bharadwaj RK. Macromolecules 2001;34:9189-9192.

[19]   Fredrickson GH, Bicerano J. Journal of Chemical Physics 1999;110(4):2181-2188.

[20]   Lape NK, Nuxoll EE, Cussler EL. Journal of Membrane Science 2004;236:29-37.

[21]   Gusev AA, Lusti HR. Advanced Materials 2001;13(21):1641-1643.

[22]   Hao J, Lewin M, Wilkie CA, Wang J. Polymer Degradation and Stability 2006;91:2482-2485.

[23]   Gilman JW, Jackson CL, Morgan AB, Harris RH, Manias E, Giannelis EP, Wuthenow M, Hilton D, Phillips SH. Chemistry of Materials 2000(12):1866.

[24]   Fornes TD, Paul DR. Polymer 2003;44:4993.

www.ingramcontent.com/pod-product-compliance
Lightning Source LLC
Chambersburg PA
CBHW080343290526
45791CB00009BA/2722